DUETS

SINGER'S *Wedding* ANTHOLOGY

A COLLECTION OF 23 DUETS, INCLUDING CLASSICAL AND TRADITIONAL, POPULAR, AND CONTEMPORARY CHRISTIAN SELECTIONS FOR ANY WEDDING OCCASION.

ISBN 0-7935-4099-2

HAL•LEONARD™ CORPORATION

7777 W. BLUEMOUND RD. P.O. BOX 13819 MILWAUKEE, WI 53213

Contents

Contents
By Category

Classical/Traditional

Contemporary Christian

Popular

Laudamus Te

from GLORIA

ANTONIO VIVALDI

te. Be - ne - di - ci - mus te.
name, Bles - sed, is Thy name.
SOPRANO II
Lau - da - mus te. Be - ne -
We praise Thy name, Bles - sed
A - do - ra - mus te. Glo - ri - fi -
We a - dore Thee, O Lord, We praise and a -
di - ci - mus te. A - do - ra - mus te.
is Thy name. We a - dore Thee, Lord.
mf
ca - - -
dore
Glo - ri - fi - ca - -
We praise and a - dore
f

mus te.
thee, Lord.
mus te.
thee, Lord.
tr
Lau - da - mus te. Be - ne - di - ci - mus te. A -
We praise Thy name, Bles-sed, bles - sed art Thou. We
Lau - da - mus te. Be - ne - di - ci mus te.
We praise Thy name, Bles-sed, bles - sed art Thou.
mf
- do - ra - mus te. Glo - ri - fi -
a - dore Thy name. Glo - ry ev - er
A - do - ra - mus te. Glo - ri - fi -
We a - dore Thy name. Glo - ry ev - er

più f
ca - mus te. A - do -
to the Lord. We a -
ca - mus te.
to the Lord.
più f
ra - mus te. A - do - ra - mus te.
dore Thy name, We a - dore Thy name.
più f
3
3
Glo - ri - fi - ca -
Glo - ry to God,
- mus te.
to God.

Lau - da - mus te. Be - ne - di - ci - mus te. A - do -
We praise Thy name, bles-sed, bles - sed art Thou. We a -
Lau - da - mus te. Be - ne - di - ci - mus te. A - do -
We praise Thy name, Bles-sed, bles - sed art Thou. We a -
mf
ra - mus te. Glo - ri - fi - ca -
dore Thy name, We a - dore
ra - mus te. Glo - ri - fi - ca -
dore Thy name, We a - dore
- mus te. Glo - ri - fi - ca -
Thy name. Glo - ry to God,
- mus te. Glo - ri - fi - ca -
Thy name. Glo - ry to God,
mf
p

- - - mus te.
to God.
- - - mus te.
to God.
mf

Panis Angelicus

(O Lord Most Holy)

CÉSAR FRANCK

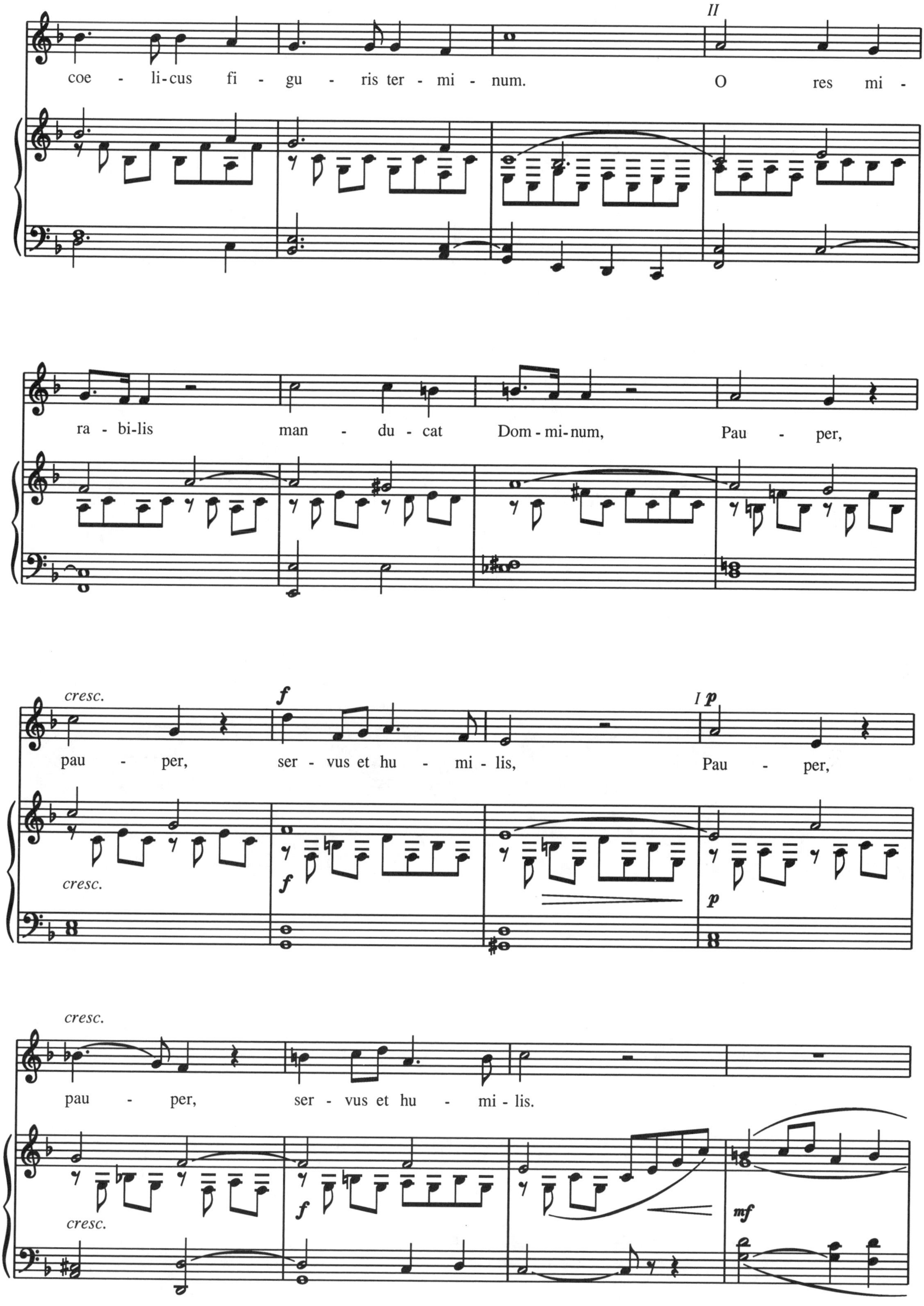
II
coe - li-cus fi - gu - ris ter - mi - num.
O res mi -
ra - bi-lis man - du - cat Dom - mi - num,
Pau - per,
cresc.
f
I p
pau - per, ser - vus et hu - mi - lis,
Pau - per,
cresc.
f
p
cresc.
pau - per, ser - vus et hu - mi - lis.
cresc.
f
mf

I mf
Pa - nis an -
cresc.
ge - li-cus fit pa - nis ho - mi-num, Dat pa - nis
II mf
Pa - nis an - ge - li-cus fit pa - nis ho - mi-num,
cresc.
f
coe - li-cus fi - gu ris ter - mi - num. O res mi -
f
Dat pa - nis coe - li-cus fi - gu ris ter - mi - num.
cresc.
f

ra - bi-lis, man - du - cat Do - mi-num Pau - per,
O res mi - ra - bi-lis, man - du - cat Do - mi-num
ff
pau - per, ser - vus et hu - mi - lis, Pau - per,
ff
Pau - per, ser - vus et hu - mi - lis, Pau - per,
I,II unison
pau - per, ser - vus, ser - vus et hu - mi - lis.
decresc.
p

Pur Ti Miro, Pur Ti Godo

By CLAUDIO MONTEVERDI

If the string quartet is used, this keyboard part should be played with the quartet, preferably on a harpsichord.

- no, non pe - no, più non pe - no, non mo -
- ing or sor - row, no more long - ing or sor -
mo - ro, più non pe -
long - ing, no more sor -
2
ro, o mia vi - ta, o mio te - so - ro,
row, o my dear - est, o my be - lov - ed,
no, o mia vi - ta, o mio te - so - ro,
row, o my dear - est, o my be - lov - ed,
cresc.
o mi - a vi - ta o mio te - so - ro.
o my dear - est, o my be - lov - ed.
o mi - a vi - ta, o mio te - so - ro.
o my dear - est, o my be - lov - ed.
decresc.

3 Allegretto
Io son tua, spe - me mia,
I am yours, all my hope
Tu son io, dil - lo,
I am yours, say to
mf - p
dil - lo, di', spe - me mia, dil - lo, di',
say to me you are mine, all my hope,
di', tu sei pur, l'i - dol mio, tu sei
me you are mine, my de - sire, you are
l'i - dol mio, tu sei pur. Sì, mio ben,
my de - sire, you are mine o my love,
pur, dil - lo, di', l'i - dol mio, sì, mio
mine, say to me, my de - sire, o my

4
mia vi - ta, sì, sì, sì, sì, sì mio cor, mia vi - ta,
my dear - est one, o my life o my life my dear - est
cor mia vi - ta sì, sì, mio ben, mia vi - ta, sì, sì, sì,
life, my dear - est one, o my love, my dear - est one, o my
(cresc. 2nd time)
1
sì, sì, sì, sì, sì, sì, mio ben, sì, mio cor, mia
one, o love, o life, o my love, o my life, my
sì, sì, sì, sì, sì, mio ben, sì mio cor, mia
life, love, o life o my love, o my life, my
vi - ta, sì.
dear - est love.
2
ben, sì, mio cor, mia vi - ta,
love, o my life, my dear - est
vi - ta, sì.
dear - est love.
ben, sì, mio cor, mia vi - ta,
love, o my life, my dear - est

5
Tempo primo
sì. Pur ti mi - ro, pur ti mi - ro,
love. I be - hold you, I be - hold you,
sì. Pur ti go - do, put ti
love. I a - dore you, I a -
mp
pur ti strin - go, pur ti strin - go, pur t'an -
let me hold you, let me hold you, and en -
go - do, pur t'an - no - do, pur ti strin -
dore you, let me hold you, let me hold
no - do, più non pe - no, non pe -
fold you, no more long - ing or sor -
- go, pur ti strin - go, più non mo -
you, let me hold you, no more long -

6 Lento
no, più non mo - ro, non mo - ro, o mia vi - ta,
row, no more long - ing or sor - row, o my dear - est,
ro, più non pe - no, o mia
ing, no more sor - row, o my
o mio te - so - ro, o mi - a vi - ta,
o my be - lov - ed, o my dear - est,
vi - ta, o mio te - so - ro, o mi - a
dear - est, o my be - lov - ed, o my
rit.
o mio te - so - ro.
o my be - lov - ed.
vi ta, o mio te - so - ro.
dear - est, o my be - lov - ed.
colla voce
rit.
rit.

Whither Thou Goest

Words and Music by
GUY SINGER

* *Normally, male voice on the higher notes, female voice on the lower notes.*

Ab Adim Eb/Bb Abm6/Cb
peo - ple shall be my peo - ple my love,
Eb/Bb F9 Bb7sus Bb7
Whith - er thou go - est I will go. For
Eb7 Bb7 Eb Eb7
as in that sto - ry long a - go, The
Ab Eb7 Ab
same sweet love sto - ry now is so. Thy

Adim
Eb/Bb
Abm6/Cb
peo - ple ___ shall be my peo - ple ___ my love,
Eb/Bb
Bb7
Gm7b5
C7
Bb/D
C7/E
Whith - er ___ thou go - est ___ I will go. ___
(I will go.)
Fm7
Bb7
Cb
Whith - er thou go - est, I will go, I will
Abm
*
Eb
go, I will go. ___

* *optional*

I will go. ___

Jesu, Joy of Man's Desiring

JOHANN SEBASTIAN BACH
Arranged by JOHN REED

Love most bright.
mu - sic rings!
Drawn by Thee, our souls as - pir - ing
Where the flock, in Thee con - fid - ing,
Soar to un - cre - a - ted
Drink of joy from death - less

light.
springs.
mf
Word of God, our flesh that fash - ion'd
Theirs is beau - ty's fair - est plea - sure,
With the fire of
Theirs is wis - dom's
p
cresc.

life im - pas - sion'd.
ho - liest trea - sure.
Striv - ing still to
Thou dost ev - er
Truth un - known,
lead Thine own,
Soar - ing, dy - ing, 'round Thy
In the love of joys un -

throne.
known.
1
Optional repeat
2

All I Ask of You

from THE PHANTOM OF THE OPERA

Music by ANDREW LLOYD WEBBER
Lyrics by CHARLES HART
Additional Lyrics by RICHARD STILGOE

Andante
RAOUL
Db
No more talk of dark - ness, for - get these wide-eyed fears; I'm
mp
Dbmaj7
Gb6
Cb
Ab/C
here, noth - ing can harm you, my words will warm and calm you.
Db
Let me be your free - dom, let day - light dry your tears; I'm

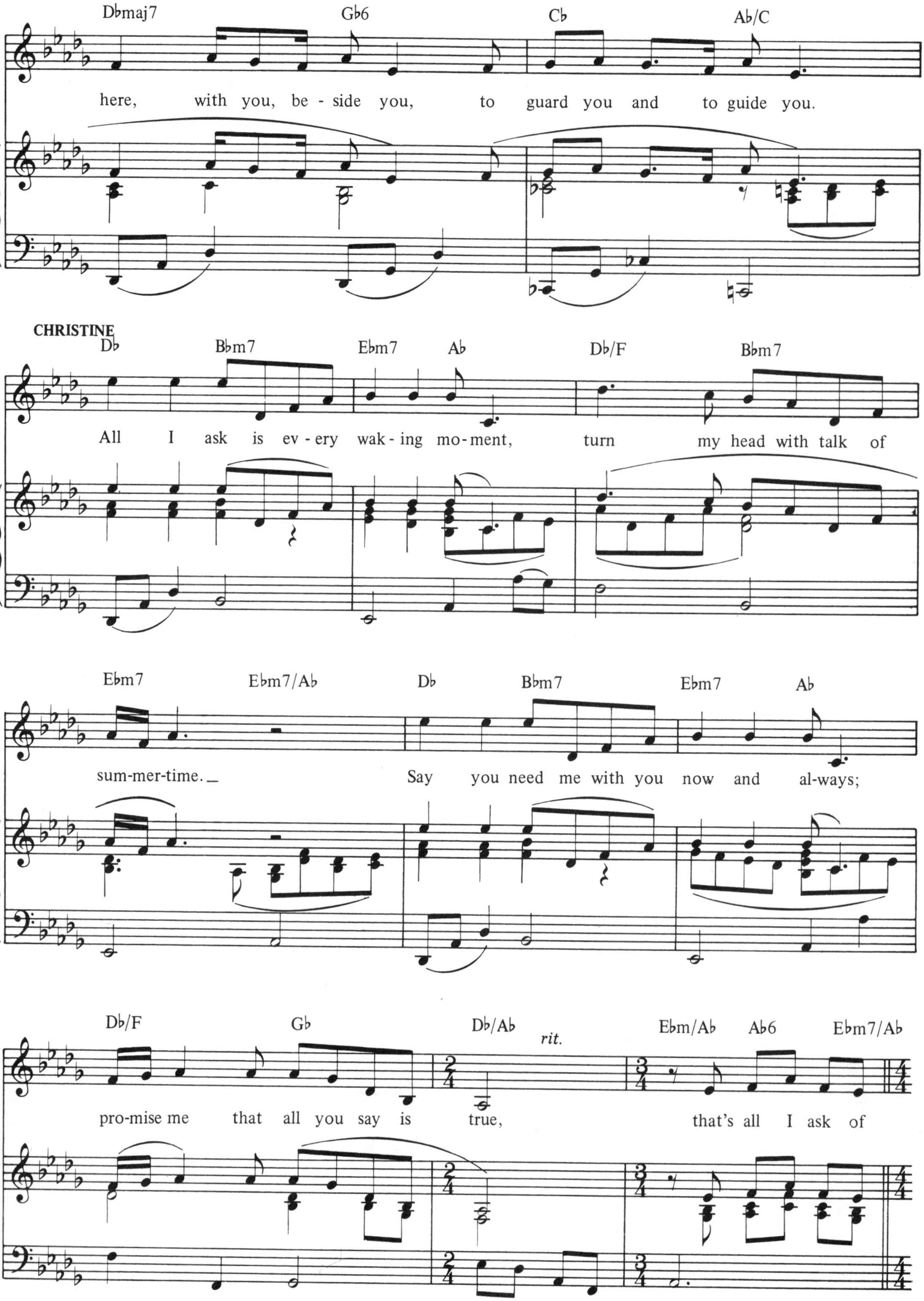
Dbmaj7 Gb6 Cb Ab/C
here, with you, be - side you, to guard you and to guide you.
CHRISTINE
Db Bbm7 Ebm7 Ab Db/F Bbm7
All I ask is ev - ery wak - ing mo - ment, turn my head with talk of
Ebm7 Ebm7/Ab Db Bbm7 Ebm7 Ab
sum-mer-time. _ Say you need me with you now and al-ways;
Db/F Gb Db/Ab rit. Ebm/Ab Ab6 Ebm7/Ab
pro-mise me that all you say is true, that's all I ask of

a tempo
RAOUL
Db
Dbmaj7
Gb6
Let me be your shel- ter,
you.
let me be your light;
you're safe,
no one will find you,
your
mf
Cb
Ab/C
CHRISTINE
Db
fears are far be-hind you.
All I want is free-dom,
a world with no more night;
and
Dbmaj7
Gb6
Cb
Ab/C
RAOUL
Db
Bbm7
you, al-ways be-side me,
to hold me and to hide me.
Then say you'll share with me one
f
Ebm7
Ab
Db/F
Bbm7
Ebm7
Ab
Ab6
Ab7
love, one life-time;
let me lead you from your so-li - tude.

Db Bbm7 Ebm7 Ab Db/F Gb
Say you need me with you, here be - side you, an- y where you go, let me go
rit. molto rit. a tempo
Db/Ab Ebm7/Ab Ab6 Ebm7/Ab Db Bbm7
CHRISTINE
too, Christ-ine, that's all I ask of you.
All I ask for is one
f
Ebm7 Ab Db/F Bbm7 Ebm7 Ebm7/Ab
love, one life-time; say the word and I will fol-low you.
Db Bbm7 Ebm7 Ab Db/F Gb
TOGETHER
Share each day with me, each night, each morn-ing.
CHRISTINE
Say
8va bassa
RAOUL
you love me!
rit.
You know I

RAOUL & CHRISTINE
molto rit.
a tempo
Db/Ab Ebm7/Ab Ab6 Ebm7/Ab Db Bbm7
do. Love me, that's all I ask of you.
f
Ebm7 Ab Db/F Bbm7 Ebm7 Ebm7/Ab
Db Bbm7 Ebm7 Ab
largo
CHRISTINE & RAOUL
Db/F Gb
An-y-where you go, let me go
f
ff
RAOUL & CHRISTINE
molto rit.
Db/Ab Ebm7/Ab Ab6 Ebm7/Ab Db
too; love me, that's all I ask of you.
mp

Annie's Song

Words and Music by JOHN DENVER
Arranged by RICK WALTERS

spring - time, like a
walk in the rain,
Like a storm in the des -
ert, like a sleep - y blue

o - cean,
You
fill up my sen - ses,
come
fill me a - gain.
mp
f
mf
Come let me

love you, let me
give my life to you,
Let me drown in your laugh -
ter, let me die in your

arms,
mp cresc.
(HE:)
Let me lay down be - side you,
f
decresc.
rit. SHE:
let me al - ways be with you,
a tempo
p rit.
a tempo
HE:
SHE:
come let me love you,

come love me a - gain.
HE:
You
fill up my sen - ses
like a

night in a for - est,
SHE:
like the
moun - tains in spring - time,
like a
walk in the rain,
HE:
SHE:
like a
storm in the des - ert,
like a

sleep - y blue o - cean, you
fill up my sen - ses, come
fill me a - gain.
rit.
a tempo
f
ff
mf
mp

The Battle Hymn of Love

Words and Music by DON SCHLITZ
and PAUL OVERSTREET

A
1
2
too.
you.
I for -
(Both:) With
D
God as my wit - ness, this
A
vow I will make: "To have and to hold
you, no oth - er to take."
To Coda

E
A
(Female:) For rich or for poor, under skies
gray or blue,
D
(Both:) till my
A
E
A
death I will stand by you.
(Male:) There are

wars and there are ru - mors.
Wars yet to come.
Temp - ta - tions we'll
E
A
have to walk through.
Though
oth - ers may trem - ble, I

D
A
will not run. Till my death, I will
E
A
stand by you. (Both:) I will
D
put on the ar - mor of
A
faith - ful - ness to fight for a heart

E
that is true.
(Male:) Till the bat -
A
- tle is won
I will not
D
rest.
(Both:) Till my
A
death I will
E
A
D.S. al Coda
stand by you.
With

CODA
E
A
rich or for poor, un - der
D
A
skies gray or blue till my death I will
E
A
stand by you. Till the bat -
A
- tle is won I will not

D
A
E
run. Till my death I will stand by
A
D
A
you.
D
A
E7
A
rit.

Don't Know Much

Words and Music by BARRY MANN,
CYNTHIA WEIL and TOM SNOW

Em7 F F/A G/B C F G
but I know I love you, and that may be all I need to
Csus C C/E Fmaj7/A G/B
Look at these eyes, they've nev - er seen what mat - ters.
know.
C Cmaj7/E F F/A G/B
Look at these dreams, so beat - en and so bat - tered.

Am Fmaj7 G Em7 Fmaj7
But I know I love you.
I don't know much, but I know I love you,
F F/A G/B C F G
That may be all I need to
and that may be all I need to
C G/B Am D7 Gmaj7 C
know.
know. So man - y ques-tions still left un - an-swered.

F F/G C G/C C Cm7 E♭/F F
And when I feel you near me
So much I've nev-er brok-en through.
B♭maj7 E♭maj9 A♭ E♭/G Fm7 E♭/G
some-times I see so clear-ly the on-ly truth I've ev-er known is me and you.
The on-ly truth I've ev-er known is me and you.
A♭maj7/B♭ B♭/D E♭(add9) E♭/G
Look at this man,

Ab/C
Bb/D
Eb
Eb/G
Look at this soul,
so blessed with in-spi-ra-tion.
Look at this soul, still
Ab
Bb/D
Cm
Abmaj7
Bb
I don't know much,
search-ing for sal-va-tion.
I don't know much,
Gm7
Ab
Ab/C
Bb/D
Eb
Abmaj7
Bb
but I know I love you,
that may be all I need to
but I know I love you,
and that may be all I need to

E♭
E♭/G
A♭
B♭
know.
know.
E♭
E♭/G
A♭
A♭/C
B♭/D
Cm
A♭maj7
B♭
I don't know much,
I don't know much,
Gm
A♭
A♭/C
B♭/D
E♭
A♭maj7
B♭
but I know I love you,
that may be all I need to
but I know I love you,
and that may be all I need to

Eb Bb/D Cm Abmaj7 Bb Gm Ab
know. I don't know much, but I know I love you,
know. I don't know much, but I know I love you,
Ab/C Bb/D Eb Abmaj7 Bb
that may be all there is to
and that may be all there is to
Ebsus Ab/Bb Eb(add9)
know.
know. Woh.
rit.

Endless Love

Words and Music by
LIONEL RICHIE

Eb
first love, you're ev'-ry breath that I take,
(r.h.)
Eb/F Fsus F Bb F/A
you're ev'-ry step I make.
And
cresc.
Eb Eb/F F Bb F/A
mp
I all my
I, I want to share all my
mp

Gm Dm/F Eb Eb/F F
love with you,
love with you, no one else
will do.
Bb Bb9 Eb
And your eyes,
mf
Your eyes, your
cresc.
mf
Eb/F F9 Bb F/A Gm7 F6
they tell me how much you care. Oh
eyes, they tell me how much you care. Oh

Ebmaj7
Dm7
Cm7
yes, you will al - ways be
yes, you will al - ways be
Eb/F
Bb
mp
my end - less love.
mp
my end - less love.
8va
mp
p
Two hearts,
Two hearts,
cresc.
mp

Eb
Eb/F
F
two hearts that beat as one;
our lives have
two hearts that beat as one;
our lives have
Bb
just be - gun.
For - ev - er
just be - gun.
Ooh,
Cm7 Bb/D Ebmaj9
Eb/F
F9
I'll hold you close in my arms,
I can't re -
I'll hold you close in my arms.
I can't re -

Bb
F/A
Eb
mf
sist your charms. And love,
sist your charms. Oh love,
mf
Eb/F
F
Bb
F/A
Gm7
F6
3
I'll be a fool for you, I'm
I'll be a fool for you, I'm
Ebmaj9
F
Bb
sure; you know I don't mind.
sure; oh, you

* Hit the note and fall away

Bb
Eb
Eb/F
Fsus F
love.
love.
Bb
mp
Bum bum
p
Love.
mp
Bum bum
mp
Cm7 Bb/D
Ebmaj9
Eb/F
F7
bum bum bum bum bum bum bum bum
bum bum bum bum bum bum bum bum

Bb Bb9 Eb
mf
bum bum bum Oh, and love,
mf
bum bum bum Oh, and love oh love,
cresc.
mf
Eb/F F Bb F/A Gm7 F6
3
I'll be that fool for you, I'm
3
I'll be that fool for you, I'm
3
Ebmaj7 F Bb
sure; you know I don't mind. 'Cause I
sure; oh, you

Bb9
Ebmaj7
Eb/F
F
f
3
don't mind. And yes, you'll be the
know I don't mind. And yes, you'll be the
cresc.
Bb
F/A
Gm7
F6
Ebmaj7
on - ly one. No one can de - ny
on - ly one. 'Cause no one can de -
Dm7
Ebmaj7
Dm7
this love I have in - side. I'll
ny this love I have in - side. I'll

Ebmaj7
Dm7
Cm7
give it all to you my love, my love,
give it all to you, my love,
decresc.
Eb/F
Bb
Cm7 Bb/D
mp
my endless love.
mp
my endless love.
mp
p
3
Ebmaj9
Eb/F
Fsus F
Cm/Bb
Bb
rit.

In My Life

Words and Music by JOHN LENNON
and PAUL McCARTNEY
Arranged by JOHN REED

Lyrically, not too slow

A
HE:
F#m
B7
HE:
Dm
HE:
SHE:
SHE:
still can re - call. _ Some are dead _ and _ some _ are _ liv-ing; in my ______ life I've
A
E7
HE:
A
C#m/G#
loved them all. _ But of all these friends and
F#m
A7/E
D
Dm
A
SHE:
C#m/E
lov- ers there is no _____ one com-pares with you, _ and those mem- 'ries lose their
F#m
A7/E
D
Dm
A
HE:
SHE:
mean- ing when I think of _ love as some - thing new. _ I

F♯m Bm G D Dm A
HE:
know_ I'll_ nev-er lose af - fec-tion for peo-ple and things_ that went be-fore,_
SHE: I
F♯m B Dm
SHE: HE:
know I'll of - ten stop and think a - bout them. In my life,
SHE: I
A E7 Very slowly Dm
love you more._ In my life, I
A E7 A
love you more.
a tempo
rall.

Let It Be Me

English Words by MANN CURTIS
French Words by PIERRE DeLANOE
Music by GILBERT BECAUD
Arranged by RICK WALTERS

G/B C/G G#dim7 Am G/A
Don't take this heav - en from one, If you must
mp
Am7 G/A Am7 G/A Fmaj7 C/E
cling to some - one, Now and for - ev - er,
3
3
Dm7 Am/G G6 C Dm7 C/E F
Let it be me. Each time we
mf
C/E Fmaj7 C/E
meet, love, I find com - plete love,

F6 C/E Dm9
With - out your sweet love, what would life
E♯5 E C G/B
be? So nev - er leave me lone - ly,
Am7 C/G F Dm7
Tell me you'll love me on - ly, And that you'll
C/E G/A Am/G Fmaj7 Am G6 C
al - ways Let it be me.
p
mf
8va

G/B Am7 Dm9 Em7 Fmaj11 F6
C SHE: G/B Am7
If, for each bit of glad - ness, Some - one must
p
C/E F6 C/E
taste of sad - ness, I'll bear the sor - row,
3
Fmaj9 G C HE:
3
Let it be me. No mat - ter

G/B
Am7
Em7
what the price is,
I'll bear the sac - ri - fi - ces,
F6
C/E
Fmaj9
F/G
G
HE:
3
Through each to - mor - row,
SHE:
Let it be
C
Dm7
C/E
Fmaj7
Em7
me.
To you I'm pray - ing,
mf
Fmaj7
C/E
Fmaj7
Hear what I'm say - ing,
Please let your

C/E
Fmaj7
E7
heart - beat for me, just me.
Am/E
E
Slower
Db
SHE:
And nev - er leave me
HE:
And nev - er leave me
f
Fm/C
F7
Bbm7
Ebm/Ab Gb
Fm
Fm7
Gbmaj7
lone - ly, Tell me you'll love me on - ly,
lone - ly, Tell me you'll love me on - ly, And that you'll

Db/F Bbm7 Ebm7 Db/Ab Ab Bbm Ab/Bb Bbm7
always Let it be me, always,
always always Let it be me,
mf
Gbmaj9 Db/F Ebm/Bb Bbm7 Ebm9 Db/Ab Ab
rit.
always, always Let it be
always, always, always Let it be
8va
Db Bbm7 Ab/Gb Gb6
me.
me.
p

Somewhere Out There

from AN AMERICAN TAIL

Words and Music by JAMES HORNER, BARRY MANN and CYNTHIA WEIL

Moderately slow, with expression

Em7 Am Dm7 C/E F Gsus G
of me and lov - ing me to - night.
C(add9) Cmaj7/E C/F F/G C(add9) C/E
(Male:) Some - where out there some - one's say - ing a prayer
F Dm7 G/F
that we'll find one a -
Em7 Am7 Dm7 C/E F/G
noth - er in that big some - where out

C
there.
And
F
G/F
e - ven though I know how ver - y
F
G/F
far a - part we are
Fmaj7
G/F
it helps to think we might be wish - in'
F
G/F
on the same bright star.
(Female:)
And
A♭
B♭/A♭
when the night wind starts to sing a
A♭
B♭/A♭
lone - some lul - la - by
A♭
B♭/A♭
it helps to think we're sleep - ing un - der -
rit.

G
C
Cmaj7/E
(Male:)
neath the same big sky.
(Female:) Some - where
a tempo
f
Fmaj9
F/G
C
C/E
F
out there it love can see us through
Dm7
G/F
3
Em7
Am7
F
then we'll be to - geth - er some-where out there out
dim.
G
C
D/C
C
D/C
where dreams come true.
mf

C/B♭ B♭maj7 C/B♭ D/E
A C♯m7 A/D D/E A A/C♯
D D+ D6 A/C♯ Bm7 Dmaj7 C♯m F♯m7
Bm7 C♯m D/E A F G/F
(Male:) And e - ven though I know how ver - y
f
dim.
mf

F G/F Fmaj7 G/F
far a - part we are it helps to think we might be wish - in'
F G/F A♭ B♭/A♭
on the same bright star. (Female:) And when the night wind starts to sing a
A♭ B♭/A♭ A♭ B♭/A♭
lone - some lul - la - by it helps to think we're sleep - ing un - der -
rit.
G C Cmaj7/E
(Male:)
neath the same big sky. (Female:) Some - where
a tempo
f

Fmaj9 F/G C C/E
(Male:)
out there (Female:) if love can see us
F Dm7 G/F
Love can see us through to -
3
through, then we'll be to -
Em7 Am F G
geth - er
geth - er some- where out there, out where dreams come
mf
rit. e dim.
C Cmaj7/E C/F G7sus C(add9)
true.
p
a tempo

True Love

from HIGH SOCIETY

Words and Music by
COLE PORTER

Note: The recording by Elton John and Kiki Dee is one half-step higher, as is our companion recording. We are printing the song in this key for playability.

HE: G7
F6
SHE:
true love, true
C HE: F F♯dim7
love. So, on and on it will al - ways
C G7 F6
HE:
SHE:
be true love, true
C Fm7 Fm7/B♭ E♭maj7
love. For you and I have a guard - ian

Cm7 Fm7 Fm7/B♭ G7
an - gel on high with noth - ing to do.
F/G HE: C F F♯dim7
But to give to you as you give to
C HE: G7 F
me SHE: love for - ev - er true,
C G7 F
love for - ev - er true.

1
C
For
2
C
Eb
Ab
Adim7
Eb
Bb7
True
love,
1
Ab
true
Eb
love.
2
Ab6
true
Eb
love.
For
Abm7
you
and
Abm7/Db
I
have
a
Gbmaj7
guard - ian
Ebm7
an - gel
on

Abm7
Abm7/Db
Bb
Ab/Bb
SHE:
high with noth - ing to do. But to
Eb
Ab
Adim7
Eb
give to you as you give to me
Bb7
Ab
Eb
love for - ev - er true,
Freely
Bb7
Ab
ad lib.
Eb
love for - ev - er true love.
molto rall.

Up Where We Belong

from the Paramount Picture AN OFFICER AND A GENTLEMAN

Words by WILL JENNINGS
Music by BUFFY SAINTE-MARIE and JACK NITZSCHE

G D7/F♯ Em7 A
The road is long. There are
D D/F♯ G G/B C D7/C C
moun-tains in our way, but we climb a step ev-'ry
A G/A A HE: D D/F♯ G Bm7
SHE:
day. Love lift us up where we be-long, where the
Em7 D/F♯ C G A
ea - gles cry on a moun - tain high.

D
D/F#
G
Bm
Love lift us up where we be - long,
far from the
Em
D/F#
HE:
F#/A#
Bm
Gm
world we know;
up where the clear winds blow.
D
G/B A/D
G/D
Gm/D
HE:
D
G/D Dmaj7
Some hang on to
G/D
Gm/D
D
G/D Dmaj7
"used to be,"
live their lives
look - ing be -

G/D Gm6/D SHE: D G/D Dmaj7 G/D Gm6/D
hind. All we have is here and now; all our
D D7/F# G D7/F# HE: Em7
life out there to find. The road is
A D D/F#
long. There are moun-tains in our way,
G G/B C D7/C C
but we climb them a step ev-'ry

A G/A A D HE: D/F#
SHE:
day. Love lift us up where we be - long,
G Bm7 Em7 D/F#
where the ea - gles cry on a
C G A D D/F#
moun - tain high. Love lift us up where we be - long,
G Bm7 Em7 D/F# HE:
far from the world we know; up where the

E7/G♯ A A/G F C/E
clear winds blow. Time goes by,
7
E♭ B♭/D D♭ A♭/C
no time to cry, life's you and I, a -
B♭ A♭/B♭ B♭ E♭ HE: E♭/G
live to - day.
SHE:
Love lift us up where we be - long,
A♭ Cm7 Fm7 E♭/G
where the ea - gles cry on a

Db Ab Bb Eb Eb/G
moun - tain high. Love lift us up where we be - long,
Ab Cm7 Fm7 Eb/G
HE:
far from the world we know; up where the
G/B Cm Abm Eb Eb/G
clear winds blow. Love lift us up where we be - long.
Ab Eb
8vb

When I Fall in Love

Words by EDWARD HEYMAN
Music by VICTOR YOUNG

A7sus
A7♭9
Dm
Gm6
gun, and too man - y moon - light kiss - es seem to
Dm
G6/B
F/G
Steadily, with feeling
C
cool in the warmth of the sun.
When I give my
Fm/C
C
Fm6/C
C7♭9
heart it will be com -
Am6/C
G7♭9
C
Dm7
Em7
Fmaj7
B♭/A
A+
- plete - ly, or I'll nev - er give my

C/D D6 Fmaj7 G7♭9
heart. Don't let me give my heart. And the
C Am7 F♯m7♭5 B7♯11 D/E A
mo - ment I can feel that you feel that way
Dm7 B♭7 C/G Gm7♭5
too, I feel that way too, is when I fall in
F/G G7♭9 C G/A
love, I'll fall in love with you.

Dm7 Fm C/D G7sus C
When I fall in
Fm6/C C B♭7 A7
love it will be for -
Dm7 G9sus C Dm7 Em7 Fmaj7
- ev - er, or I'll nev - er
B♭/A A+ C/D D6
fall in love, oh, I'll nev - er, nev - er fall

Fmaj7/G
G7♭9
C
Am7
in love.
In a rest - less world like
B♭7♯11
C
Gm/B♭
A7sus
A7♭9
this is,
love is end - ed be - fore it's be - gun,
and too
Dm7
Dm(maj7)
man - y moon - light kiss - es
seem to
Dm
A9sus
cool in the warmth of the sun.

D
Gm/D
When I give my heart
D
C7
B7
Em7
A7
it will be com - plete - ly,
D
Em7
F#m7
Gmaj7
C/B
B7♭9
or I'll nev - er give, I'll nev - er give my heart,
D/E
E6
Gmaj7/A
A7♭9
oh, I'll nev - er give my heart. And the

D
Bm
A/G
C#7♭9
mo - ment I can feel that you
F#m7
B7♭9
Freely
Em7
C9
feel that way too is
D/A
Gm6/A
D7♭9/A
E7/A
Gm6/A
F/C
B♭m6/C
F7♭9/C
G7/C
B♭m6/C
when I fall in love, when I fall in love,
D/A
Gm6/A
D7♭9/A
Bm6/A
A
D
E/D
Gm6/D
D
when I fall in love with you.

A Whole New World

(Aladdin's Theme)

from Walt Disney's ALADDIN

Music by ALAN MENKEN
Lyrics by TIM RICE

Moderately, sweetly

2
E♭
B♭
F
ma - gic car - pet ride. A whole new world
B♭
F/A
B♭
B♭/D
a new fan - tas - tic point of view. No - one to
3
F/E♭
B♭/D
F/E♭
B♭/D
Gm7
C7sus
C7
tell us no or where to go or say we're on - ly
E♭/F
F
B♭
dream - ing.
Female: A whole new world a daz - zling

F F#dim7 Gm Bb7 F/Eb Bb/D
place I nev - er knew. But now from way up here it's
F/Eb Bb/D Gm7 C7sus C7 Abmaj9 F7sus
crys - tal clear that now I'm in a whole new world with
Bb Db
you. Un - be - liev - a - ble
Gb/Bb Ab/C
sights in - de - scrib - a - ble feel - ing.

E♭m/G♭ F7 B♭m A♭ G♭
Soar - ing, tum - bling, free-wheel - ing through an end - less dia - mond sky.
D♭ A♭ D♭
A whole new world a hun - dred
Male: Don't you dare close your eyes.
A♭ D♭ G♭ D♭/F
thou - sand things to see. I'm like a shoot - ing star. I've
Hold your breath, it gets bet - ter. I'm like a shoot - ing star. I've

G♭ D♭/F B♭m7 E♭7 G♭/A♭
come so far. I can't go back to where I used to be.
come so far A whole new
A♭ D♭ A♭/C Adim7
world with new ho - ri - zons to pur - sue.
B♭m D♭7/A♭ G♭ D♭/F G♭ D♭/F
I'll chase them an - y - where. There's time to spare.
I'll chase them an - y - where. There's time to spare.

B♭m7
E♭7
C♭maj9
G♭/A♭
A
Let me share this whole new world with you.
F♯m7
Bm7♭5
E7sus
E7
Bm/D
C♯7
3
F♯m
F♯m/E
Gmaj9/A
F♯m7
A7/C♯
A whole new world.
A whole new

D
A7/C#
D
No - one to
world_ a new fan - tas - tic point_ of view.___ No - one to
G
D/F#
G
D/F#
Bm7
E7sus
E7
tell us no or where to go___ or say we're on - ly
tell us no or where to go.___
G/A
A
D
dream - ing. Ev - 'ry turn a sur - prise.___
A whole new world with new ho -

A/C# A#dim7 Bm D7/A G D/F#
Ev - 'ry mo - ment red let - ter. I'll chase them an - y - where. There's
ri - zons to pur - sue. I'll chase them an - y - where. There's
G D/F# G9#11 F#m7 F#7/A# Bm7
time to spare. An - y - where.
time to spare. There's time to spare.
Bm7/E E9 Cmaj9 G/A Bm
Let me share with you. Ooh.
this whole new world you.
rit.

G#m7♭5
no chord
F#m7
G
F#m7
A whole new world, that's where we'll be.
A whole new world, where we will
a tempo
G
F#m7
G/A
A7
D
A thrill-ing chase for you and me.
be. A won-d'rous place for you and me.
rit.
a tempo
Gmaj7/B
A/C#
D
rit.

All I Long For

Words and Music by
CHARLIE PEACOCK

Moderately (♩ = 82)

Note: This is basically the arrangement recorded by Susan Ashton and Michael English, but the vocal parts have been adapted for a live duet performance.

G A Bm G A
All I long for, found in
D5 G A D5
You. Sweet mer - cy,
G A D5 G A
grace and peace, All I
Bm G2(no3) A7sus
1.
D5 D
long for, found in You.

2.,3.
D2(no3)
SHE: G A D5
You.
Here I am, teach me true,
HE:
Em/G D/G A D5
SHE:
All I long for found in you. Sweet mer - cy, grace and peace,
G2(no3) A7sus Bm G A
All I long for, found in
D2
2nd time To Coda
G A D
You.

G A D
G A
Bm G
A A7
D
G A
D5
G A
HE: Je - sus Christ,
Ho - ly
D5
G A
Bm
G
One,
All I long for,

A A7 D5
D.S. al Coda
found in You.
CODA
HE: G A D G A D
SHE: Here I am, teach me true,
G A Bm G
All I long for,
A A7
1. D
Repeat ad lib.
2. D
found in You.
You.

Commitment Song

Words and Music by ROBERT STERLING
and CHRIS MACHEN

(I and II)
bless our sol - emn vow__ That as long as we're__ to - geth-er__ the name of
give us when__ we stray__ Lead us back with ten - der mer-cy__ with Your
Db2 Db Ab2/C Ab/C Cm7/F F9
Je - sus will__ be raised
pre - cious love__ and grace.
(mel.)
O__
Abmaj7/Bb F/G G/B
Lord, dear Lord, we praise Your ho - ly name.__ We're
(unis.)
C2 C G/A Am7 Fmaj9 F6 Dm7 E7/G#
stand-ing here__ to - geth - er to mag - ni - fy__ the Son.__ Let our
(mel.)
Am Am/G F#m7(b5) F/G G/B

(unis.)
lives and our love show the world why Je - sus came. Let them
C2 C G/A Am7 Fmaj9 F6 Dm7 E7/G#
know His love has made us one, made us
Am Am/G Dm7 Fmaj7/G
1. one.
2. one.
(Solo II)
We'll
Fm7/B♭ C2
fol-low You wher-ev - er You lead us to - geth-er we'll serve You.
(Solo I)
(Solo II)
We'll
Dm7 C2/E Dm7 C2/E

(I and II unis.)
be a light wher-ev - er You need us So let this song of praise be a
Dm7
C2/E
Fmaj7
prom - ise Lord, to You.
mel.
O
F♯m7(♭5)
G7sus
Gmaj7/A
Lord, dear Lord, we praise Your ho - ly name.
(unis.)
We're
D2
D
A/B
Bm7
Gmaj9
G6
Em7
F♯7/A♯
stand - ing here to - geth - er to mag - ni - fy the Son.
(mel.)
Let our
Bm
Bm/A
G♯m7(♭5)
E7/G♯
G/A
A/C♯

(unis.)
lives and our love show the world why Je - sus came. Let them
D2 A/B Bm7 Gmaj9 G6 Em7 F#7/A#
1. 2.
(mel.)
ritard
know His love has made us one. O Made us
Bm Bm/A Em7 G/A Gmaj7/A Em7 Gmaj7/A
ritard
ritard
one.
D A/B Bm7 G G/A D2
ritard

To Have and To Hold

Words and Music by
ROY E. BRONKEMA

A♭/D♭ D♭ E♭m9 A♭7sus A♭7
sick-ness and health, to love till death do us
D♭sus D♭ A♭/D♭ D♭ Fm7
MALE SOLO:
part. I take thee to be my
G♭ E♭m7 A♭7 D♭ G♭ D♭maj7
wed-ded wife. I'll keep you for all of my earth-ly life to
D♭ Fm7 G♭
love and hon-or and cher-ish you. I

E♭/G
G♭m6
Fm7
B♭m
G♭maj7
E♭m7
give you my life as I say, "I do." and pledge these vows un-to
A♭7
E♭m7
A7
D
F♯m7
G
FEMALE SOLO:
you. I come to you now as my earth-ly king. I
Em7
A7sus
A7
D
G
A
D
F♯m7
glad - ly will yield to you ev-'ry-thing. O-be - dient-ly, rev - 'rent-ly,
G
E/G♯
Gm6
F♯m7
Bm
trust-ing you, I give you my heart for my whole life through, and

Gmaj7 Em7 A7sus A7 B♭7sus B♭7 B♭/E♭ E♭
DUET: (male take higher notes)
pledge these vows un - to you. To have and to hold from
Gm7 Cm7 A♭maj7 Fm7 G♭maj7 Fm7 B♭7
this day forth, for bet - ter or for worse. for
B♭/E♭ E♭ B♭/C Cm7 Fm9 B♭7
rich - er, poor - er, in sick-ness and health, to have till death do us
E♭sus E♭ B♭/C C7sus C7 C/F F
part. To have and to hold from

Am7 Dm7 B♭maj7 Gm7 A♭maj7 Gm7 C7
this day forht for bet - ter or for worse. For
C/F F C/D Dm7 Gm9 Gm/C A7
rich - er, poor - er, in sick-ness and health, to love till death do us
Dm Gm7♭5 F/C Gm7 F/A Gm/B♭ B♭/C C7
part. To love till death do us
Fsus F C F
part!
R.H.

Household of Faith

Words by BRENT LAMB
Music by JOHN ROSASCO

With warmth (♩ = 66)

Abmaj7 Bb/Ab Gm7 C Fm7 Ab/Bb Bb/Ab
SHE:
house - hold of faith that to - geth - er we can make, and when the strong winds blow it won't fall
Gm7b5 C7 Fm7 Ab/Bb Bb/Ab Gm7 C7sus C
down. As one in Him we'll grow and the whole world will know
Fm7 Ab/Bb Bb Eb Fm7(4) Eb2/G Fm7
we are a house - hold of faith.
E SHE: F#m7 Emaj7/G# A E F#m7
Now, to be a fam - i - ly, we've got to love each oth - er at an - y cost un - self - ish -
mf

E/G# F#m7 A/B Emaj9 F#m7 G#m7 G#7♭9 G#7
ly. And our home must be a place that full-y a-bounds with
C#m E/F# F#m7 A/B Amaj7 B/A
HE: mf
SHE:
grace, a re-flec-tion of His face. We'll build a house-hold of faith that to-
mf stronger
G#m7 C# F#m7 A/B B/A G#m7♭5 C#7sus C#7
geth-er we can make, and when the strong winds blow it won't fall down. As
F#m7 A/B B/A G#m7 C#7sus C#7 F#m7 A/B B
one in Him we'll grow and the whole world will know we are a house-hold of

E Bb/C Bbmaj7 C/Bb Am7 D
f
faith. We'll build a house - hold of faith that to - geth - er we can make and
Gm7 Gm7/C C/Bb Am7b5 Dsus D
when the strong winds blow it won't fall down. As
Gm7 Bb/C C/Bb Am7 Dsus D
3
one in Him we'll grow and the whole world will know
Gm7 Gm7/C F2 Gm7 Fmaj7/A Bb2 F2
mp rit. a tempo rit.
we are a house - hold of faith.

I.O.U. Me

Words and Music by BENJAMIN WINANS, KEITH THOMAS,
TOM HEMBY, MIKE RAPP and BILLY SPRAGUE

Med. Fast 4 (half-time feel)

A
you
I could see that it was me
Dmaj9
you came to find
E
by the smile that was on
A
your face.
Male
Oh,
and the pain
Fmaj7
C
B♭
Dm9
Bm7
E
in my heart
met the love
in your eyes
and
opt.

A
Female
Bm7/E
went a-way. When you told
A
Male
3
Female
me (when you told me) it was true what you went through
Dmaj9
3
E
I tried to thank you, but it was some-thing no words
A
Male
(opt. 8va lower)
Dm6/A
Female
could do. (no words) I owe love

CHORUS
A F♯m7 E/D D A/D E/D C♯m7 F♯m7
all my love I owe ev - 'ry-thing to you. All of my life
I owe love all my love ev - 'ry-thing to you. All of my life
Male
Bm7 Dm/F A/E Bm7/E A F♯m7
you've giv - en love to me. I owe love all my heart it be-longs
you've giv - en love to me. I owe love all my heart it be-longs
E/D D A/D E/D C♯m7 F♯m7 Dm/F F2
to on - ly you the rest of my life.

Bm7/E
A
I know I. O. U. me.
Male
Bm7/E
A
Ev-'ry mo - ment
(opt. 8va lower)
3
Dmaj9
'till the world no long-er turns could I re-pay you,
A
but I've found a way to start.

Fmaj7
Male
Oh,
ev-'ry day,
ev-'ry day,
ev-'ry night
Female
Female
C/B
Dm9
Bm7/E
this is what I write up-on my heart.
A
Dm6/A
I owe love,
We both know
Male

A
Male
Duet
E/D D A/D E/D
all my love,
I owe ev - 'ry - thing to you.
I owe love,
all my love,
Female
C♯m7 F♯m7 Bm7 Dm/F A/E Bm7/E A
Male
All of my life you've giv-en love to me. I owe love,
I owe love
Female
F♯m7 E/D D A/D E C♯m7 F♯m7
Male
Duet
all my heart, it be - longs to you
the rest of my life.
it be - longs to on - ly you

Dm
F
F2
Bm7
E
I know I. O. U. me.
A
D
A
A
Bm
A
A
E
I know I. O. U. me.
A
Dmaj9 C♯m7
Repeat and fade
Repeat and fade

Love's Not a Feeling

Words and Music by STEVE CAMP
and ROB FRAZIER

Gmaj7 Asus Em9 Gmaj7 D9(no3)
we wash our hands of it so eas-i-ly,
when the pres-sure's on and times are tough.
Dm9 Em9 Fmaj9
We give up so fast and then won-der why love does-n't last.
Just trust in His pow'r; He'll see you through your dark-est hour.
F/G
HE:
SHE:
C Am7
Love's not a feel-in', oh, we've got to learn; to
Fmaj7 Dm9 F/G D
get past our e-mo-tions to the mean-ing of the word. Love's not a feel-in' we can

Repeat on D.S. only
Bm7
Gmaj7
D2/F♯
Em7
G2/A
lose or throw a - way.
Lord, give us the cour - age to live it ev - 'ry day.
1.
To Coda
Em9
Asus/B
A
Em9
Asus/B A/B
2.
Em9
Bmaj9
Asus
Em9
HE: There's a
(ad lib. Sax solo)
Gmaj7
D9(no3)
Dm9
Em9
Fmaj9